Advance praise for
Stress Reduction for Lawyers, Law Students, and Legal Professionals

"This is the best book written about the value of mindfulness and meditation for lawyers as well as others in high-stakes occupations. Its author combines expertise in the law, contemplative practice, and clear writing. He gets right to the point, with examples, specific suggestions, and focused experiential practices. The ideas and tools in it will replace stress with greater calm, resilience, and well-being."

**—Rick Hanson, PhD, author of *Resilient* and
*Buddha's Brain***

"Stephen Snyder shares practical wisdom, born of his experience as a lawyer and his remarkable insight into the interchange between mindfully based stress relief, Buddhist thought, and his true compassion for others. He has lived what he writes in this book and has done so with honesty and grace. As a psychologist, I wholeheartedly recommend this incredibly important book, not only for lawyers but for all of us."

**—Judy F. Kennedy, PhD, licensed psychologist and
business consultant**

"I found this book enlightening for its simple advice. I'm an Italian civil lawyer and I empathize very much with the difficulties and challenges described. I met Stephen at a retreat he led and I did some of the practices described in the book. They changed my point of view, made me more aware, and allowed me to be kinder to myself and others—not all the time but as much as I can. The precious advice gifted through this book has the same purpose and I really loved it."

—Vanessa Camerano Spelta Rapini, civil lawyer, Italy

"Stephen Snyder's book is the distillation of decades of wisdom, matured in the crucible of lived experience. Stephen writes with lucidity, drawing the reader's attention to the essential and transformative practices of stress reduction through meditation, listening, and techniques for heart-based awareness. This small gem of a book offers insight and science-informed practices that can make a difference here and now. Stephen is a wise teacher generously opening his heart so those who practice the art of law might do so with their full selves and with greater enjoyment."

—The Rev. Kevin G. Thew Forrester, PhD, St. Stephen's Episcopal Parish

"This is a must read for all attorneys. Frankly, it should also be required reading in all law schools. While most seminars and books focused on stress and substance dependency in the legal profession only address the causes of legal work–related anxiety and stress, Mr. Snyder's book provides substantive help and exercises that go well beyond just identifying the problem.

As a trial attorney with hundreds of active cases, a father, a husband, and a youth sports coach, I often feel like I am being pulled in multiple directions. This book is simply the best literature I have digested to go beyond identification of stress for attorneys and explain how to actually make changes to address the issue."

—Neil Berman, trial attorney

"Stephen Snyder is a skilled litigator who is also trained in traditional Buddhist meditation techniques. In this excellent book, he draws on his own experience in the law, where he recognized that stress is often an outcome of difficult or combative relationships, whether they're with clients, colleagues, or opposing counsel. He found that adopting an authentic and openhearted approach to such relationships dramatically changed them from stressful encounters to positive interactions. In his book, he has shared easy but powerful practices that will help lawyers achieve similar outcomes."

—Derek Broadmore, retired barrister, New Zealand

"*Stress Reduction for Lawyers* is a brilliant book—short enough to be read quickly and thorough enough to be life changing. This book will help you to improve your relationships with clients, colleagues, and judges. Beyond this, it will help you to improve your relationship with yourself as you learn to lower your stress level and begin to enjoy your life more fully."

—Marcia Cannon, PhD, MFT, author of *The Gift of Anger*

"This book succinctly brings together the naming of stressors unique to those in the legal profession with antidotes for these challenges—including helpful exploratory exercises to emotionally connect with one's self and others—and timeless, simple meditation practices that can be readily practiced by anyone to reduce stress, increase focus, open the heart, and cultivate equanimity. These practices are described completely enough for any reader to be able to put down the book and begin them successfully. I would recommend this book not only to lawyers but to anyone trying to cope with stress and its related challenges."

—Heather C. Young, clinical psychologist and meditation teacher

"Stephen's new book is a superb guide to stress reduction and meditation. It takes the tried-and-tested ancient techniques of meditation and presents them in a modern format that is concise and easy to understand. When the instructions and exercises are applied and practiced then surely they will lead anyone to a calmer and more contented life, lawyer and Buddhist monk alike."

—Ñānavira, Matthew Buckley, Buddhist monk

"*Stress Reduction for Lawyers* by Stephen Snyder is a precious gem of a book. Stephen calls on his experience, both as an attorney and a skilled meditation teacher, to succinctly produce evidence-based, practical advice aimed at increasing the well-being of lawyers.

As a psychotherapist, I appreciate the skill with which Stephen, while being realistic about the challenges of running a legal practice, has been able to communicate the benefits of emotional intelligence and stress reduction. As a mother of a successful solicitor, I am grateful for this book, which will support my son to achieve balance in his work life and to protect his health."

—Roz Broadmore, psychotherapist, New Zealand

"I worked with Stephen as a paralegal the year after his car accident, while he was struggling with post-concussive syndrome. Though the accident had a profound impact on his life, Stephen was always pleasant, serene, and focused. This book has helped me to understand how he achieved that and, in doing so, has helped me learn how to achieve it myself. I highly recommend this book for anyone dealing with high stress, whether it's due to career or life circumstances. It will help readers in tough times, and throughout life, to open their minds to more rewarding experiences."

—Elizabeth Woods, independent paralegal

"I have had the honor of welcoming Stephen to lead many meditation retreats in Italy. His guidance as a teacher has been invaluable. His book offers the same precision, simplicity, and effectiveness of his in-person teachings. It is also very dear to me since my partner is a lawyer and I have the privilege of observing the legal world from the inside. I hope these practices will be undertaken by as many lawyers as possible as they have the power and the knowledge to change people's lives. These practices give readers the best way for making that change."

—Andrea Magoni, web designer, Italy

STRESS REDUCTION

for Lawyers,
Law Students,
and Legal
Professionals

STRESS REDUCTION

for Lawyers,
Law Students,
and Legal
Professionals

Learning to Relax

STEPHEN SNYDER

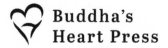

Buddha's
Heart Press

Buddha's Heart Press
www.workingforbalance.com

Library of Congress Control Number: 2020911227
ISBN 978-1-7347810-0-7 (paperback)
ISBN 978-1-7347810-1-4 (e-book)

Editing by Erin Parker
Proofreading by Lynn Slobogian
Cover and interior design by Jazmin Welch
Project management by Carra Simpson

Contents

13 *Who I Am and Why I Wrote This Book*

21 *Some Common Causes of Stress
in the Legal Profession*

29 EXERCISE ONE: Your History and
Relationship with Stress

31 *Assessing the Effects of Stress*

38 EXERCISE TWO: Unhealthy and Healthy
Responses to Episodes of Stress

41 *An Introduction to Meditation*

49 *Focused Attention Stress Reduction
(FASR)*

54 EXERCISE THREE: FASR Meditation

59 *Recognizing Emotions to Become a Better Listener*

64 EXERCISE FOUR: Learning to Recognize Emotions

70 EXERCISE FIVE: Inattentive Listening

73 EXERCISE SIX: Attentive Listening

77 *Heart-Based Practices*

81 EXERCISE SEVEN: Equanimity

85 EXERCISE EIGHT: Being with Your Innate Goodness

89 EXERCISE NINE: Loving-Kindness to Others

91 *Putting It All Together*

97 Notes

99 Other Resources

101 Acknowledgments

Who I Am and Why I Wrote This Book

HAVING WORKED AS A LITIGATION LAWYER for a number of decades (first in California and now in Michigan), I am quite familiar with the demands that clients, opposing counsel, and the courts place upon legal professionals. There is too much to do in the allotted time. And if they make a mistake or do not win the case, lawyers face serious consequences. This all contributes to a high-stress atmosphere.

When my legal career began, I initially felt I needed to keep my meditation practice and spiritual life separate from my work life. I was of the mind that if I fully incorporated my spiritual life into my legal work, I would be too soft, too agreeable, and liable to be taken advantage of by more assertive lawyers. A few years into my legal career, I realized I wasn't managing my stress sufficiently. I was unable to shut off my thoughts about work dynamics. I was neither present to my family, attentive to friends, nor able to relax during time off. I was carrying this stress into all aspects of my life and letting it plague my sleep and downtime. After a court appearance in which I was so mentally exhausted that I was fumbling my client's legal arguments, I finally realized something had to change. What I was doing in separating my spiritual life from my professional life wasn't helping, and my stress level was consistently increasing.

I was of the mind that if I fully incorporated my spiritual life into my legal work, I would be too soft, too agreeable, and liable to be taken advantage of by more assertive lawyers.

Soon after, I began to intentionally employ meditation, greater emotional intelligence, and deeper listening to align my approach to work with my core values. Really, this meant bringing all of me—all of who I was—into every area of my life. The removal of any artificial separation between my personal and professional life supported work-life balance and my effectiveness as a lawyer. My work life became enjoyable and satisfying. Clients liked interacting with me more, I did better in litigation, and I felt more congruent with my core values. I was also able to relax both during and after work. I was happier!

While practicing as a lawyer, I attended spiritual retreats ranging in length from days to months. In 2004, I was able to arrange my schedule such that I could attend a two-month silent meditation retreat with one of the foremost meditation masters in the world. It was a demanding retreat doing deep "concentration meditation," also called "focused attention meditation." During this retreat, I completed around forty different meditations to the level of mastery, as witnessed and validated by my meditation teacher, the Venerable Pa Auk Sayadaw. I was one of the first Western men, and the first American man, to complete the *samatha* portion of the traditional Buddhist path. My teacher encouraged me to write a book of my experiences aimed at a Western audience. I cowrote *Practicing the Jhānas* with another student from the retreat, and the book was published by Shambhala Publications in 2009. The *jhānas* are the deepest level of concentration available in meditation. It is a rarefied field with no thinking, no sense of a personal "I," and the ability to spend hours in silent, rejuvenating meditative realms.

In 2007, after completing the book and beginning to lead retreats and work with students, I was authorized as a lineage meditation teacher by one of the most widely respected and revered meditation masters in the world, the Venerable Pa Auk Sayadaw. Part of my training consisted of interviewing students on retreat while being mentored by this meditation master. Since then, I have—individually or with a teaching partner—taught retreats throughout the US, in Europe, and in the UK. I have also worked individually with students on a spiritual path, offering one-on-one coaching and guidance.

With my lawyer hat on, I now do presentations on stress reduction and offer coaching to those in the legal profession who wish to deepen their meditation practice, be supported in their spiritual unfoldment, and achieve greater life balance and work satisfaction. (Please see my website, www. workingforbalance.com, for further information.)

To effectively improve one's stress levels and work-life balance, it's important to understand how stress develops, how each of us naturally tries to cope with stress, and what unhealthy outlets we may choose to try to numb ourselves from the effects of stress. That's our starting point in this book.

Then, after a short introduction to meditation, we will explore specific techniques we can employ right now to give us some space, some distance, some ease, and a place to decompress. We'll try out Focused Attention Stress Reduction (FASR) and look at some of its benefits.

Next, I offer some exercises for improving understanding of our own and others' emotions, and listening skills, which pave the way for more authentic communications and interactions.

Finally, I'll lead you in some easy heart-based meditation practices: "Equanimity," "Being with Your Innate Goodness," and "Loving-Kindness to Others." Each of these practices add a way for us to develop greater capacity to be with the difficulties of life, be directly in touch with our more serene nature, and just be happier in general.

Some Common Causes of Stress in the Legal Profession

LAWYERS ARE MOSTLY UNSEEN, usually unacknowledged, pillars of modern society. Like each of you, I struggled to manage the pressures of modern law practice. I found that stress about cases and income affected my quality time with family. I was regularly intruded upon by my worry and an inability to thoroughly put down my workload at the end of the day. I also found myself consuming more and more caffeine as I made an effort to stay up and focus. It will be no surprise to learn that the caffeine didn't work as intended and that my efforts did not reduce my stress level.

In the legal profession, I see three areas of ongoing stress we deal with regularly: 1) interpersonal conflict and misunderstandings; 2) heavy workload and time pressure; and 3) the high-stakes nature of the work.

> *I was regularly intruded upon by my worry and an inability to thoroughly put down my workload at the end of the day.*

Interpersonal Conflict and Misunderstandings

When individuals and families are in dire need of help with divorce, adoptions, real estate transactions, wills and probate, criminal charges, contract disputes, personal injury claims, and many other issues, they turn to lawyers. Often anxious and overwhelmed, clients want their legal situations fixed quickly and inexpensively. When there are unforeseen circumstances, factual discrepancies, or unexpected delays, clients can become frustrated and impatient. Lawyers sometimes bear the brunt of these negative feelings.

Interacting with clients is one source of interpersonal stress; communicating with other legal professionals, court personnel, colleagues, and staff is another. Sometimes there are unexpected changes to opposing counsel, the opposing law firm, or the judge assigned to the case. You might have a good working relationship with the original opposing counsel only to find yourself suddenly working with a lawyer with whom you don't see eye to eye, communicate effectively, or get along.

Heavy Workload and Time Pressure

There are also ongoing tensions in trying to accept, and maintain, the amount of work coming in the door, allocating it equitably among law firm personnel. I was not alone in taking on too many cases to comfortably handle. My concern was that if I turned away work, my clients would begin to look elsewhere to assign all of their cases.

> *I was not alone in taking on too many cases to comfortably handle.*

Then there's the fact that each case involves many tasks: drafting the needed legal documents, communicating with and managing multiple people, and effectively juggling the many demands for meetings and court appearances, among other jobs. This adds to time-management pressures. Also, cases that appear to be easy, requiring not much work, usually become the more demanding cases. The unpredictability of the factors affecting the difficulty of a case added a lot to my stress level.

If we were able to do an established amount of work that didn't increase or get more challenging, stress would be manageable. Like much of life, legal work takes more time than allotted and relationships prove more challenging under pressure to succeed without faltering or failing.

One common strategy to manage excessive work is to multitask. My attempts to do several tasks at once, such as talking on the phone while composing written documents, appeared to help with the workload demands. But, as we will see later in this book, multitasking actually adds time to our work by making us less efficient and effective in both of the multitasking efforts.

We may also try coming in early and/or staying late when others are not present to lessen in-person demands on our time. While this can be effective, it also reduces the time we spend with our loved ones, causing more stress.

High-Stakes Work

In the legal profession, court deadlines, statute of limitations, client expectations, and supervisor or firm billing requirements all compete for the lawyer's time. Couple the time demands with lawyers' tendency to be less developed in interpersonal communications, particularly talking about emotional feelings, and all this leads to great stress. Lawyers carry the worry that if they make a significant mistake in their professional life, it can mean a negative job review, malpractice claim, and/or bar discipline. Perhaps worst of all, it could mean bad, even life-changing, outcomes for their clients. This puts additional pressure on legal professionals.

On top of stress-inducing interpersonal relationships, a heavy workload, and the serious consequences of making a mistake or failing, let's not forget that there can be other unforeseen events that occur outside of work that nonetheless complicate our professional lives. At one point in my career, I was in a bad car accident. It left me with a significant concussion. One negative effect was that, for a couple weeks, I miscalendered court hearings to the wrong year! I did not realize it until I began getting notices from the different courts threatening sanctions for missing court appearances. Fortunately, when I explained what had happened, the opposing counsel and judges were quite understanding. There are many sources of stress in our lives, some more difficult to anticipate than others.

In order to better manage our stress, we have to be clear about our history and relationship with it.

In order to better manage our stress, we have to be clear about our history and relationship with it. In other words, we need to ask ourselves, "What is my pattern in meeting and trying to manage stress? Which of my strategies and coping mechanisms are working and which are not?" To better identify your history with stress, I have a brief exercise for you.

EXERCISE ONE

Your History and Relationship with Stress

What are the specific areas of stress in your professional and personal life? (Some examples: "Too many phone calls," "An excessive number of firm meetings," "Too large a caseload," "Difficult opposing counsel," etc.)

_____

_____

_____

_____

_____

_____

_____

All these work-related demands that legal professionals face, along with family and personal responsibilities, lead to increased stress levels. Fortunately, by reorienting our life balance, refocusing on our values, and learning some relaxation techniques, we can lessen our stress, which results in greater happiness and increased life satisfaction.

To fully understand how to manage stress, we need to recognize its effects and our responses to it, which is the focus of the next chapter.

Assessing the Effects of Stress

STRESS IS A NATURAL REACTION to being psychologically overloaded by too much information and too many demands, in a limited period of time. Possible responses include a perception of dread and a growing feeling of inadequacy or failure. Accurate self-assessment is the first gift you can give yourself in this stress reduction program. If

> *Accurate self-assessment is the first gift you can give yourself.*

you feel significantly overwhelmed, it may be best to speak with a health-care professional. In this book, we are working with a minimum to moderate level of stress. Doing an informal self-assessment is not a replacement for medical diagnosis or treatment. Below are some reactions to stress and/or common coping behaviors used in attempts to manage stress.

- **Excessive substance use**—drinking too much alcohol; using prescription or nonprescription drugs solely to relax or numb the feeling of pressure
- **Change in sex life**—having lowered or excessive libido; acting inappropriately toward others; obsessing over sex or porn
- **Fatigue/tiredness**—feeling run-down or chronically lethargic despite resting and getting sleep
- **Sleep difficulties**—having trouble falling or staying asleep, when this isn't usually a problem
- **Irritability/frustration/anger**—reacting to interruptions or unexpected, unwelcome change with impatience or anger; lashing out at people you care about over trivial events or actions
- **Anxiety/worry/overexcitement**—experiencing circular thinking of what could go wrong; feeling disproportionately amped up in response to life and work demands
- **Depression/hopelessness/deep sadness**—feeling despondent when reviewing your life and work demands; having difficulty letting go of hopeless or helpless feelings; feeling a crushing weight of responsibility
- **Digestion issues**—overeating/bingeing; refraining from food or water; regularly eating unhealthy

food; experiencing chronically upset stomach or gastrointestinal issues, with or without medical causation

- **Body tension/headaches**—experiencing body discomfort, without medical causation; feeling ongoing muscle tension or fatigue; experiencing excessive head pain or tension; feeling ongoing muscle tightness
- **Restlessness**—having difficulty sitting without frequently changing your body position; foot tapping or leg shaking; experiencing racing thoughts or excessive energy in body or mind
- **Difficulty focusing**—needing to reread book passages or paperwork; not taking in what people are saying to you directly; routinely forgetting what you are intending to do; making simple mistakes due to inattention
- **Excessive stimulation**—routinely ingesting too much caffeine or other stimulants; shopping or buying pleasurable items without true regard for need; distracting yourself through internet or TV
- **Unusual level of withdrawal**—pulling back from loved ones or activities that historically give you pleasure; refusing or minimizing participation in

social engagements; experiencing a desire to hide from life's demands

As you review this list of potential reactions to excessive stress, you may feel inner recognition and be better able to identify which of these you experience.

One way to see these patterns more clearly is to observe yourself on vacation. In what areas of life do you see yourself acting excessively? Do you sleep better with fewer worrying thoughts about work? How are you feeling overall? These types of questions will help you see the difference between your vacation and work stress levels and give you insight into the effectiveness of your coping techniques.

There is plenty of statistical and anecdotal evidence that many legal professionals experience the signs of stress listed above. For example, a 2016 study published in the *Journal of Addiction Medicine* concluded that 19 percent of lawyers suffer from ongoing anxiety, 21 percent are "problem drinkers," and 28 percent struggle with depression.[1] When I was in law school in the 1980s, I became aware that some students used cocaine as a stimulant in order to feel mentally sharp enough to keep up with the heavy workload. While practicing law, I have been to hearings and depositions where I could smell alcohol on the breath of another attorney. These and other addictive substances may make us feel as though we are veiled from our life and work stressors, when in fact we are simply numbing ourselves and clouding our minds, leaving us less effective in our work and more distant in our relationships.

> *Addictive substances may make us feel as though we are veiled from our life and work stressors, when in fact we are simply numbing ourselves and clouding our minds.*

Early in my career, I was working on a complicated case with a number of attorneys. One attorney in particular would show up late to depositions, miss counsel meetings, and appear in court barely prepared for the hearing. He was an attorney with many years of experience who enjoyed a very good professional reputation. I finally had to confront him about how his style of practicing law was negatively affecting my client and other clients in the case. It turned out he had developed a serious drinking problem. He readily got help, which greatly benefited his life and his work.

To more fully understand how you manage stress, try this exercise.

EXERCISE TWO

Unhealthy and Healthy Responses to Episodes of Stress

PART ONE

What are some *unhealthy* ways you have responded to a stressful period or event? (Some examples: "I drank too much coffee," "I significantly increased my hours in the office at the expense of my family life," etc.)

_____

_____

_____

_____

_____

_____

_____

PART TWO

What are some *healthy* ways you have responded to a stressful period or event? (Some examples: "I went for a walk at lunch," "I talked to a close friend," "I went to the gym to burn off excess energy," etc.)

_____

_____

_____

_____

_____

_____

_____

Personal stress can also be measured using an instrument called the "Perceived Stress Scale." (Please see the Other Resources section for more details.)

An Introduction to Meditation

I WAS FIRST INTRODUCED to stress reduction and relaxation exercises through meditation. I began meditating in 1976. At that time, I did not understand how I fit in the world or what my contributions would be, I felt concerned about a lack of meaningful relationships, and I wondered what form my career might take.

I chanced upon a book that outlined a number of meditation techniques and practices. I tried most of them and settled on a few. Some of the meditations were called "concentration meditation." This means directing your awareness to specific meditation objects, such as your breath. Other meditations I came to learn included heart meditations.

The first time I meditated I could only sit still for five minutes. Those five minutes were a challenge to not squirm! In that first meditation, I felt a sense of inner grounding that was unfamiliar. This supported my desire to continue with meditating. Being shy and introverted, I did not tell anyone I had started meditating. A few months later, people at work were telling me that I regularly appeared calm and relaxed. Internally I felt a little different but not dramatically so. I learned that the benefits of meditation work slowly to modify our consciousness. We enjoy the benefits even if we

> *All meditations train us to quietly turn within. It is not a turning away from our life but rather tuning in to our interiority to more fully be present in our everyday activities.*

aren't aware, on an intellectual level, about the inner changes that have already occurred.

All meditations train us to quietly turn within. It is not a turning away from our life but rather tuning in to our interiority to more fully be present in our everyday activities. In most meditations we are bringing our awareness to a specific meditative object. The meditative object is different in each type of meditation.

Meditation has an interesting set of benefits. Our psychological structuring, our personality, and our ego can be improved and matured through staying with a meditative object despite the demands—the pulls—of our minds. For example, while meditating, you may have a memory of the past. If you stay with your meditation, rather than spending time participating in or reliving the memory, the muscle of meditative concentration will strengthen. Next time, you will be able to stay with your meditation more easily. Stress reduction techniques, such as meditation, can naturally contribute to a felt sense of serenity with a mood of tranquility. Serenity reduces the pull of depression and anxiety, allows you to be more content when alone, improves relationships by letting you be more present with others, and increases overall life enjoyment.

Meditation is not the cure-all for all stress. You want a balance in meditation, too. It's useful to cultivate your interpersonal relationships and maintain physical exercise and body health habits, while ensuring you enjoy sufficient time away from work.

Brain researchers identify four types of meditation:

1 **Focused attention meditation (concentration meditation)**—Focused attention meditation involves directing your awareness to a specific meditative object to the exclusion of all mentalizing or body sensation. It is electing the object of meditation, such as the breath, over every distraction that is not the breath.

2   **Open monitoring meditation (insight/ mindfulness/*zazen*)**—This is a meditation that involves opening your awareness to everything in your present-moment experience without rejecting anything. You direct your awareness to whatever is dominant. But rather than participating in, or engaging with, each thought that arises, it is recommended that you label or note the activity in awareness. For example, if you are experiencing a lot of thoughts, you would label these "thoughts." Using a label softly neutralizes the mental function and helps you to not engage with each and every thought. If you are experiencing back soreness, you would use the label "pain" rather than ruminating on what caused the injury, how long you've had it, etc. Continuing in this way, we eventually reach a stage where the mind calms, the need for labels quiets, and we can just *be* with the open awareness itself, perceiving everything that passes without engaging with it.

3   **Heart-based meditations, such as loving-kindness (*mettā*) and compassion (*karuṇā*)**—This series of meditations supports intimacy with the depths of your heart. We commence these meditations on more of a surface layer. By "surface layer," I

mean our everyday ordinary perspective—how we usually view the world and ourselves. Through sustained practice, our awareness descends past our memories, our life history, and our beliefs about emotional issues to reach a place of more universal, objective heart qualities of what Buddhists call "our deeper nature." This is our core personal reality that has been masked by social conditioning and life history. In doing these heart practices, we develop the ability to have our heart present not just to ourselves but to others in a healthy, wholesome manner.

4 **Self-transcending (*cittānuppasanā/rigpa*) meditation**—Self-transcending experiences are always outside our personality view. We are fully aware yet not overly identified with our usual sense of self, our personality. These meditations support the ability to move outside—beyond—our usual sense of self. They open us to universal, objective experiences of inner reality without the ever-present personality patterning or egoic functions. These meditations open our awareness from a more limited, personal view to an expanded, universal perspective. We may see ourselves as an undivided part of a wholeness encompassing

the entire universe. Or we might know we are a wave upon the undivided ocean of life. Self-transcending meditation is usually combined with focused attention meditation to concentrate our awareness to the point where our awareness shifts quite naturally from ordinary mind to an awake awareness that is ever present. These meditations are more advanced.

In this book we will focus on two areas of meditation: 1) focused attention meditation, using the Focused Attention Stress Reduction (FASR) meditation, and 2) heart-based meditations, which help us to be more intimate with our deeper heart qualities. We will be using an innate-goodness practice to locate and welcome the unconditioned goodness in us. Sustained contact with knowing our goodness brings us unending joy. We will also employ an equanimity (*upekkhā*) meditation to develop greater smoothness of mind and inherent balance, and a loving-kindness meditation to cultivate tenderness of heart toward ourselves and others.

Focused Attention Stress Reduction (FASR)

FOCUSED ATTENTION MEDITATION involves concentrating on a solitary object to the exclusion of all other mental, psychological, or physical distractions. It is choosing to rest your awareness on a particular object (in this case, your breath), rather than following wherever your mind naturally wanders.

Focused attention meditation can counteract chronic distractions, and help you stay focused on one activity and be more present to others in a relational way, while reducing compulsion and addiction to the internet and electronic forms of communication.

FASR has the following benefits:

1   Helping us stay calm under increasing pressure
2   Increasing clarity in decision making
3   Improving sleep
4   Boosting our immune system
5   Increasing positive emotions while reducing negative emotions
6   Improving relationships as we become more present and better listeners

7   Supporting reprogramming of the brain to reduce emotional reactiveness and rumination

8   Helping us develop greater satisfaction with life as it is

9   Increasing gray matter in the brain, which can lead to enhanced learning, emotional regulation, and empathy

10   Supporting greater brain neuroplasticity[2]

With sustained, regular meditation, we can counteract the effects of the three categories of stress we examined earlier—interpersonal conflict, heavy workload and time pressure, and the high-stakes nature of work in legal professions. We will enjoy relaxation and restfulness, have fewer angry reactions, calm our worries, lighten our mood, smooth tensions in our body, and achieve greater focus. This will lessen our stress on an ongoing basis.

FASR can also help lawyers under intense work pressure who try to cope by multitasking. Brain researchers have confirmed that when we engage in multitasking, also called "task switching," we lose time acclimating to the new task. Our cognitive functioning slows as we switch tasks, particularly if they're complex. Rather than being more efficient by multitasking, we are less efficient at all the tasks we are trying to juggle.[3]

Regular focused attention exercises can decrease the time it takes to readjust between tasks. While I'm not advocating for multitasking, it is helpful to know that when we are interrupted from our current task, we can develop the ability to quickly resume our work with the help of sustained stress reduction exercises.

Let's take a moment to slow down and practice FASR.

EXERCISE THREE
FASR Meditation

> Sit comfortably with your feet flat on the floor and your back in an upright yet relaxed posture.

> Your head should be level, not tilted up or down.

> Rest your hands comfortably in your lap.

> Close your eyes.

> Let go of thoughts, emotions, memories, judgments, and opinions.

> Remain present and attentive.

> Feel yourself sitting in your chair.

> Feel the support the chair provides.

> You are being held.

> *Breathe, and know you are breathing in this moment.*

> You may notice the breath either as it passes between the nostrils and the upper lip or in the movement of the belly—rising and falling with each breath.

> Being with the breath is your most important action right now.

> Feel any sense of ease or relaxation. Let it spread through your body and mind as it wishes.

You have just completed a session of FASR!

Reflections

How was that for you? Can you identify any positive results from practicing FASR?

_____

_____

_____

_____

_____

_____

_____

_____

You may begin to notice that your mind is starting to unify, to cohere. With FASR, we are intending to focus awareness on one object—in this session, on the breath—to the exclusion of all else. That doesn't mean we stop our thoughts or cease emotions. We simply elect to not give those thoughts or emotions our attention, when these are present.

Are you struggling? Learning to focus our attention takes time. We can nonetheless see its benefits fairly quickly. It helps each time we undergo FASR and particularly each

> *Our "muscle" of concentration needs to be strengthened just as a body muscle would after a period of neglect.*

time we turn away from the intruding thought, emotion, memory, or judgment and return to the breath as our meditative object. Our "muscle" of concentration needs to be strengthened just as a body muscle would after a period of neglect. We start with small weights with a few repetitions and increase as we gain strength and stability. An important point is that we are not trying to eliminate thoughts, just let them be present. Imagine the passing thoughts are clouds drifting lazily across an open blue sky. We don't need to stop each cloud and name it, be chummy with it, or fully understand it. We can simply notice the cloud passing across the sky while remaining with the breath.

With increased application of FASR, your ability to concentrate will develop and strengthen. Perhaps you will start by regularly doing a ten-minute FASR session. Over time that can increase to twenty to thirty minutes or more per session. Using FASR allows us to develop the ability to stay with an activity rather than be derailed by random thoughts and compulsive mental patterning.

Can't feel your breath? This is one of the most frequent comments I hear at this point. This is understandable since we rarely slow down and turn away from our near-constant thoughts and accompanying mentalizing. With sustained practice, you will feel/sense your breath. Over the years of teaching this practice, I have witnessed that everyone who stayed with this breath meditation practice was able to fully feel their breath.

Being with the breath is our primary activity in FASR. We are actively prioritizing being with the breath over *everything* else. When a thought or a visual or auditory event momentarily captures your awareness, gently bring yourself back to being with the breath. Being with the breath is like being with a dear friend. Although there can be an interesting dialogue, even laughing, there are also occasional gaps in the conversation. Due to the level of comfort between friends, there is no push to fill the silence. Ultimately, being with the breath will also feel natural like this, unforced.

It can be helpful to undertake FASR in a quiet location with minimal distractions or interruptions. Lower, softer lighting will help you relax your eyes. But you do not want to be so comfortable that you get sleepy. That is too relaxed!

Because you are electing to bring your awareness repeatedly back to the breath, it gives your mind one task. This allows other portions of your mind to be at ease and relaxed, giving you a sense of peacefulness, tranquility, and serenity. This is the antidote to stress.

Recognizing Emotions to Become a Better Listener

I BELIEVE THAT LEGAL PROFESSIONALS, as a group, minimize the emotional experience while working. This is done in part to maintain an analytical mindset as we seek an intellectual resolution of legal disputes. It also insulates the legal professional from feeling the suffering and grief with which their clients are likely struggling. There is a prevailing belief that a successful lawyer resists the influence of any display of emotions. In reality, however, being removed from our emotions and others' makes us less able to fully perceive the human dynamics of interpersonal interactions. When we can be with our emotions, in a mature manner, we can make significant contact with clients, witnesses, staff, and opposing counsel. As a result, we'll be understood better, and believed and liked more, and our stress will diminish.

This has certainly been my experience. When I started practicing law, I wanted to fit in with the other lawyers. I felt insecure and slightly incompetent. I tried my best to only pay attention to others with my mind and to listen as a lawyer, categorizing arguments and preparing responses/rebuttals. After a few years of this, and once I felt a little more landed in the work, I began to experiment with how I behaved and how I listened. I allowed more of my personal style to mix with my professional work. I let myself be more humanly present and authentic.

I'd had a fear that if I was in touch with my emotions more and let those be seen, I would be less effective as a lawyer. In fact, the opposite was true. The more authentic I was and the deeper I listened to others, while tracking everyone's emotions, the better I did as a lawyer. Clients responded well and referred more work to me. Most other attorneys interacted with me with greater ease. I began to

> *I'd had a fear that if I was in touch with my emotions more and let those be seen, I would be less effective as a lawyer. In fact, the opposite was true.*

develop positive professional relationships with opposing counsel, which lead to better communications in which each side could be clear and zealous making their clients' arguments, while remaining professional, even collegial. We listened to each other and usually resolved our cases amicably.

I still represented my clients vigorously, yet I knew to not take the client and legal positions personally. Typically, lawyers are known to be more head centered than heart/ emotion centered. Being more head centered can minimize how in touch with emotions one can be. The better we know our own emotions, the easier it will be to understand other's emotions. Understanding another's emotions leads to greater contact and develops a personal relationship.

In this chapter you will learn how to make contact with your emotional self, begin to recognize the emotions of others, and apply these skills to listening more fully. Being more familiar with our own emotions, being more real, leads to greater ease accompanied by relaxation. This is just one of the benefits of developing your emotional intelligence (EQ).[4]

The first step in recognizing emotions is reading the emotions in faces. When we pay attention to, and understand, facial expressions, we can receive solid, reliable information about our emotions as well as another's emotional state.

Dr. Paul Ekman, a leader in recognizing facial expressions, says that all people, regardless of cultural differences, make essentially the same expressions for the same emotions. This is even true of the blind.[5] There are seven emotions that Dr. Ekman identifies as being universal: happiness, sadness, fear, contempt, anger, disgust, and surprise.

EXERCISE FOUR

Learning to Recognize Emotions

PART ONE

> Go to a mirror where you have some privacy.

> Face the mirror with your eyes closed.

> Remember a time when you were really, really happy.

> Slowly open your eyes.

> What do you notice?

> Your mouth will be turned up, the facial muscles will be lifted upward, and the forehead may look relaxed. You may see a sparkle in your eyes!

> Now go back to a neutral face.

> With eyes open, feel the happiness again.

> Do you recognize the happy face in the mirror?

> Then, once again facing the mirror with eyes closed, remember a time when you were really sad.

> Let the memory wash over you.

> Slowly open your eyes.

> What do you see?

> Your mouth is probably turned down, and the muscles in your face may appear to be drooping. There may be a flat affect to your entire face.

> While watching the mirror, let the sad memory come forward into your awareness.

> This is what sad looks like.

When you are ready, either now or at a later date, repeat this exercise with the rest of the seven emotions listed earlier.

Reflections

As you do these exercises, what do you notice about your face? How can you tell which emotion you are feeling?

_____

_____

_____

_____

_____

_____

_____

_____

I recommend that you practice this at least once a week for two months. This exercise will help you more accurately recognize not only your emotions but also others' emotions as you interpret their facial expressions.

PART TWO

> After two to four weeks of facial expression recognition practice, choose one emotion, like happiness, and notice when you see someone whose face appears to be exhibiting that emotion. How could you tell? Was their mouth turned up, were their eyes sparkling, and did their forehead look relaxed?

> Once you have developed the nonverbal skill of understanding another's emotions, you can take the next step: appropriately commenting upon a recognized facial expression. Again, start with the positive emotions like happiness.

> If you're interacting with someone and you see the facial signs of happiness, say to them, "You look happy" and then ask, "Did I get that right?" Check with the other person to see if you read their emotion accurately. Make sure you are in a happy or pleasant mood yourself. Otherwise, your dour mood may affect theirs.

Reflections

How was that experience for you and for the person you interacted with?

_____

_____

_____

_____

_____

People feel more connected with someone who can recognize and comment on what they are processing emotionally. This is true of clients, colleagues, and other legal professionals, all of whom will trust you more if they feel seen. Another benefit of developing greater emotional intelligence is that you'll be able to pick up on the unvarnished reactions of people you're communicating with. Often what we say does not match how we feel, and having the ability to read faces will put you at an advantage in the courtroom, the office, and even at home.

Finally, by improving your recognition of your own and others' emotions, you will also deepen relationships with family and friends. These close connections relieve stress, allowing you to relax.

Listening

Now that we have some understanding of the importance of emotional intelligence as well as how to employ it in our day-to-day lives, we can take an additional step. We are going to improve our ability to listen. This will support our connections with others as well as lessen tension and disagreement in our communications.

In my legal career, I often witnessed lawyers in a court setting or in conversation appear to be simply waiting for their turn to talk. They were listening enough to intellectually analyze the speaker's argument, but they were really not hearing the other person's communication.

We have all had the experience of attempting to communicate something important, only to feel as if the other person is barely listening. It's so frustrating! It can even result in hurt feelings. We may feel simply ignored or entirely dismissed. Not a pleasant experience nor a relationship-building exchange. Moreover, our message is probably not well received or heard. So, at least in part, it's a failed communication. Here are two exercises that show the effects of inattentive and attentive listening on both parties in a conversation.

EXERCISE FIVE
Inattentive Listening

PART ONE

> Ask someone you know fairly well to do a brief experiment with you. Tell them you want them to talk to you about something that's important to them for two minutes. The topic can be anything. Let them know you will purposely *not* be listening well to them.

> As the other person speaks, feel as closed to their communication as possible. Avoid looking at them. When they finish, spend some time reflecting on the exercise together.

Reflections

How did your friend find that exercise? How was it for you?

_____

_____

_____

_____

_____

_____

_____

_____

You will likely hear it didn't feel good. They probably felt unheard and rejected by you.

PART TWO

> This time, reverse the roles. You will speak about a topic that is important to you for two minutes. Ask the other person to try to be closed to you and to avoid looking at you much.

Reflections

How did it feel emotionally for you? Did you feel your message was received? Were your feelings hurt?

_____

_____

You can see from this two-part exercise what it feels like to be listener and speaker when the listener is not attentive or present.

EXERCISE SIX

Attentive Listening

PART ONE

> This time, have your friend speak for two minutes about another topic they care about. Keep fairly steady eye contact with them. Really pay attention to them and what they are saying. Listen with your whole body, including your heart. Not just with your head!

Reflections

How did your friend find that exercise? How was it for you? Did they feel attended to and really listened to? How was your understanding of their sharing? Do you feel you understood them, as a person, better than in the prior exercises?

_____

_____

_____

_____

_____

_____

_____

_____

PART TWO

> Switch roles. Speak for two minutes about a topic you care about. Ask your friend to maintain fairly steady eye contact with you. Ask them to listen not just with their head but with their whole body.

Reflections

How was that? Did you feel heard? Did you feel they "got" you and your communication? How do you feel now knowing someone really, deeply listened to you?

_____

_____

_____

_____

_____

_____

_____

_____

You can easily see, and feel, from these exercises that when the listener is attentive and connecting with the speaker, both people have a better experience. I include these exercises so you can see how opening to others supports closer interpersonal contact and, at the same time, reduces your stress level.

When we are better listeners, we can more quickly recognize when our communication isn't being received. Rather than continuing on with a discussion that is not landing, we can use greater listening skills to hear the other person and learn why our communication isn't being received as we intended. Conversely, we will be more able to fully listen to others when they're speaking and let them know their communication—their sharing—is important and valued by us. We all want to have real human contact and to be listened to by people we care about.

If you take this on as a daily practice, you will feel more real in your life and more satisfied by the interactions you have with others, regardless of the nature of the relationship.

Heart-Based Practices

BY DEVELOPING A FASR PRACTICE, you'll reduce stress and improve personal relationships by becoming more present and able to concentrate. FASR can be complemented by some easily learned heart-based practices. While most meditations positively affect our heart area, there are some that focus on profoundly softening rigid hearts and promoting authentic connection with others in your life. Both equanimity and loving-kindness are designated as heart practices. These two practices will help you really feel the struggles of others and ensure you have something meaningful to offer them.

Equanimity as Stress Reduction

To fully understand equanimity practice, we need a short introduction of how karma works. The term "karma" is used to explain the universal law of cause and effect. It can be summarized with the expression "We reap what we sow." The way we conduct ourselves, the manner in which we live and practice law, has a certain impact and effect on the people around us. They will respond to us and our behavior in fairly predictable ways. If we are thoughtful and responsible in our speech and actions, we are likely to experience others as responding favorably to us and respecting us. If, on the contrary, we are untruthful and try to manipulate others, it's likely we will be mistrusted by those around us.

We are all accustomed to witnessing the natural cause and effect of life. When someone drives too fast for road conditions and speed-limit signs, it is no surprise when they cause a traffic accident. As legal professionals we can invest our energy in trying to shape and create a certain result for our client. Yet, we need to also understand there is a natural cause and effect (karma) working, too. Understanding that there are forces working outside our control can help us to accept when a case doesn't go our way.

Understanding the workings of karma can support our acceptance of what is actually happening in our lives. For this reason, equanimity, as a spiritual practice, is used to see the natural balance of life and welcome the functioning of karma. Developing equanimity encourages us to have a more balanced, more accepting perspective. It is seeing what is naturally happening as an expression of cause and effect as truth.

EXERCISE SEVEN

Equanimity

> In a quiet place, consider someone you know
> who you feel neutral about (a store cashier,
> for example). This is someone you feel mildly
> pleasant towards simply because you do not
> know them well. It's helpful to see them
> and their life as a natural result of cause
> and effect—of karma—before turning your
> attention toward your life.

> Internally repeat the phrase "Each person is
> heir to their karma." This means this neutral
> person lives and behaves in a particular manner.
> Others in their life will likely respond to them
> according to their behavior.

> Feel the sense of internal balance and rightness
> that we are each "heir to our karma."

> Keep repeating the phrase as you picture this
> neutral person.

> Once you get a stable, internally felt sense of
> the balance and rightness of that person

receiving exactly what they sow, shift to considering yourself.

> Picture yourself in your mind's eye.

> Repeat the phrase "We are each heir to our karma."

> Consider truthfully how you live and how you practice law. Do you try to cut corners to gain an advantage or are you a straight shooter?

> While internally repeating the phrase "We are each heir to our karma," be with the felt sense of balance.

> Understand that how your life is unfolding bears a direct relationship to how you conduct yourself.

> Feel the fairness of that dynamic universal law.

Reflections

How was that for you? Can you identify any positive results from your first equanimity practice?

_____

_____

_____

_____

_____

_____

_____

_____

Loving-Kindness as Stress Reduction

Let's also explore using FASR with loving-kindness. Loving-kindness is a heart quality that is personal as well as universal. This means we can improve our own heart relationship as well as connect more easily with others in meaningful inter-personal relationships.

One factor that contributes to stress is being too involved with our thoughts—our mentalizing—and not including our heart connection. The practices outlined in this book, such as loving-kindness, will support you in making more direct contact with your heart and including it in more decisions in your life. You will probably find that the more you include the intelligence, or the knowing, from your heart, the more balanced and connected you will feel, reducing your stress.

Loving-kindness using FASR starts with opening to and getting in contact with your innate goodness.

> *The more you include the intelligence,*
> *or the knowing, from your heart,*
> *the more balanced and connected*
> *you will feel.*

EXERCISE EIGHT

Being with Your Innate Goodness

> To understand the goodness we want to make contact with, think of a newborn child. There is a sweetness they exude that is not dependent on anything they say or do. It does not require them to be efficient or effective but to simply be themselves.

> Now look for the innate goodness in yourself. Some people will be able to touch into that goodness by thinking of the people they are today. For others, it may be easier to imagine a younger version of themselves. It doesn't matter what age you feel yourself to be; what is important is to feel that innate goodness resonating internally.

> Let your awareness rest in your goodness.

> Many people feel this goodness in the area around their heart. Some find it useful to place their right hand over their heart as they reflect and rest in their own innate goodness.

> As you sense into your goodness, making contact with it, let the goodness radiate throughout your body and mind using your relaxed breathing. The goodness can ride on the movement of breath throughout your body and mind. It can also radiate in its own fashion to areas of your body and mind where it is needed most. Let your breath become comfortably relaxed.

> Using longer, deeper breaths, let your body and mind relax as much as possible.

> Pay attention initially to how your body feels sitting or lying down.

> Notice how you feel a sense of support and holding.

> Relax into that feeling of being held and supported.

Reflections

How was that for you? Could you feel your own goodness? What did it feel like? What was surprising or unexpected about sensing your own goodness? Do you feel any changes within from direct contact with your goodness?

_____

_____

_____

_____

_____

_____

_____

Direct and sustained contact with our innate goodness helps us feel settled and happy in our own skin, in our life. This can increase our sense of value and loosen the connections between our work successes and our self-worth, so that our internal sense of value is not strictly tied to our professional outcomes.

I suggest you complete this exercise twice a day at a minimum: once upon awaking for ten to fifteen minutes and again before sleep for the same amount of time. It would also be useful to do this exercise during a break in your day.

Once we can sense our innate goodness and be open to loving-kindness filling our heart and soul, we can direct it toward another.

EXERCISE NINE

Loving-Kindness to Others

> Feeling loving-kindness in your heart, seek out simple human contact with another. Try to interact with someone who is fairly neutral to you (a cashier, a receptionist, or a postal worker, for example).

> While interacting normally with them, let your heart-mind be aware of their innate goodness.

> See how your contact with loving-kindness in your heart affects the interaction with another person.

Reflections

How satisfying was the contact and communication to you? Was it different than a normal interaction?

_____

_____

_____

_____

_____

_____

_____

_____

You can see from this simple example that when you meet someone you don't know with a full heart, you can have very satisfying interactions and feel nourished by the human contact, rather than drained, which may have been your experience in the past.

Over time and with continued engagement of FASR loving-kindness, you will be able to have greater meaningful contact with many people in your life. Developing loving-kindness for another allows us to both fill our heart and soul with our innate goodness while opening and extending our heart to another. This will allow you to be real with others, feel your own heart, and reduce your stress by lessening experiences of isolation.

Putting It All Together

WE HAVE EXAMINED some causes of stress, some ways stress can manifest itself, and the roles that Focused Attention Stress Reduction (FASR), emotional intelligence, deep listening, and heart-based practices all play in reducing our stress and letting us connect with ourselves and others.

You are on your way to becoming an authentic person who can successfully recognize and manage life and work stress more effectively.

You may feel hesitant to actually try any of these practices in your regular life—the real world. If so, start small with baby steps. First try these exercises in a safe environment for very short periods of time.

What this all comes down to is being more present to, and with, yourself. As you start to relate to yourself in a more authentic way, you will naturally want to apply this same authenticity to interactions with colleagues, friends, and family. This will translate to better communications with clients, opposing counsel, and court personnel.

You are on your way to becoming an authentic person who can successfully recognize and manage life and work stress more effectively.

If you want to learn more or obtain support as you explore these new ways of being, please visit my website: www.workingforbalance.com.

I am available for presentations of this material to your bar association, law school class, firm, or group. In addition, I offer daylong workshops. Finally, I offer one-on-one coaching for legal professionals wanting individualized support learning and implementing these ways of being into their work and personal life.

Notes

1   Patrick R. Krill, Ryan Johnson, and Linda Albert, "The Prevalence of Substance Use and Other Mental Health Concerns Among American Attorneys," *Journal of Addiction Medicine* 10, no. 1 (January/February 2016): 46–52, https://doi.org/10.1097/ADM.0000000000000182

2   See Richard J. Davidson and Antoine Lutz, "Buddha's Brain: Neuroplasticity and Meditation," *IEEE Signal Processing Magazine* 25, no. 1 (January 2008): 176, https://www.ncbi.nlm.nih.gov/pmc/articles/PMC2944261/?

3   See "Multitasking: Switching Costs," American Psychological Association (March 20, 2006), http://www.apa.org/research/action/multitask. Moreover, Nancy K. Napier, PhD, concludes that the "start/stop/start process" of shifting tasks in multitasking "is rough on us. Rather than saving time, it costs time (even very small micro seconds). It's less efficient, we make more mistakes, and over time, it can sap our energy." See Napier, "The Myth of Multitasking," *Psychology Today* (May 12, 2014), https://www.psychologytoday.com/ca/blog/creativity-without-borders/201405/the-myth-multitasking

4   According to Travis Bradberry, "People with average IQs outperform those with high IQs 70 percent of the time." This is due to those average IQ individuals having a higher emotional intelligence (EQ). "Ninety percent of top performers are also high in EQ." Fortunately, EQ can be learned while IQ cannot be learned! See Bradberry, "Emotional Intelligence—EQ," *Forbes* (January 9, 2014), https://www.forbes.com/sites/travisbradberry/2014/01/09/emotional-intelligence/#7d88dc231ac0.

5   See Paul Ekman, "Universal Facial Expressions of Emotion," *California Mental Health Research Digest* 8, no. 4 (Autumn 1970): 151–158, https://www.paulekman.com/wp-content/uploads/2013/07/Universal -Facial-Expressions-of-Emotions1.pdf.

Other Resources

Perceived Stress Scale

This is a no-cost instrument that you can access online at www.mindgarden.com/132-perceived-stress-scale. It's a way to put into perspective how stressed you actually are. It's best to take the assessment without too much deliberation or anticipating the "right" answer. Scores ranging from 0–13 are considered to be low stress; scores of 14–26 would be moderate stress; and scores of 27–40 would indicate a high-stress life.

Checklist: Depression

For greater insight into your mental health, consider completing this checklist online: www.newharbinger.com/psychsolve/checklist-depression

Alcohol and Drug Abuse Self-Assessment

If you feel you may have a substance abuse issue, there are many online private assessments to help you explore your usage and its effects. Here's one I recommend: www.health. mil/Military-Health-Topics/Conditions-and-Treatments/ Assessments/Alcohol-and-Drug-Abuse-Self-Assessment

Counseling and Therapy

If you feel you are carrying too much stress, if depression is an ongoing serious problem in your life, or if you have substance abuse issues, there are counselors and therapists to help. Here's one online resource: www.samhsa.gov/find -help/national-helpline. You can also call 1-800-662-4357.

Acknowledgments

I would first like to thank my teachers and mentors for their kind patience, their attention to detail on the topics they've mastered, and their confidence in me.

Thank you also to my family for their support and encouragement, particularly my wife, Julie, who was steadfastly supportive and read each improved version of the manuscript.

A special thanks to Tina Rasmussen, with whom I developed the FASR technique at a time when we were coteaching.

Finally, thanks to Carra Simpson, Erin Parker, Jazmin Welch, and Lynn Slobogian for their essential expertise, unflagging support, and wisdom in seeing this book to publication.

About the Author

STEPHEN SNYDER was raised in Guam and in and around Hawaii. He graduated from the University of Oregon School of Law and was admitted to the State Bar of California in 1987. He practiced civil litigation, actively litigating personal injury–related cases in trial courts throughout California. In 2018, he sold his law practice and moved to Michigan, where he was admitted to the state bar in 2019. In addition to working as an attorney, Stephen has acted as a mediator in civil cases since 1990. He brings an extensive knowledge of litigation tensions and dynamics, as well as emotional and psychological blocks, to the resolution of disputes.

Authorized as a lineage meditation teacher by the Venerable Pa Auk Sayadaw, Stephen has led retreats through the US, in Europe, and in the UK since 2007. *Practicing the Jhānas*, his first book on meditation (coauthored with Tina Rasmussen), was published in 2009. He offers one-on-one coaching, short presentations, and daylong workshops on stress reduction. Please visit www.workingforbalance.com for more information.

Did you benefit from Stress Reduction For Lawyers?

SHARE YOUR PRAISE

Did this book help you manage your stress? Did it offer a new approach for managing the challenges of your work and home life? If so, a review, shared through your favorite online retailer, would be warmly welcomed. A few minutes of your time could help others find this book and benefit as you have.

PLACE A BULK ORDER

Would you like to share this book with a group? Please be in touch! We can offer bulk discounts for orders of ten or more copies to most locations. Write to buddhasheartpress@gmail.com.

KEEP IN TOUCH

For more about Stephen's books, workshops, and other offerings please visit www.workingforbalance.com.

Also by Stephen Snyder

Buddha's Heart

Meditation Practice for Developing

Well-Being, Love, and Empathy

PAPERBACK • 978-1-7347810-2-1 • $14.95

E-BOOK • 978-1-7347810-3-8 • $9.95

PUBLISHING IN JANUARY 2021

A guidebook for traversing the core Buddhist practices of the heart: the *brahmavihāras*, or four divine abodes. *Budhha's Heart* offers instruction on purifying mindfulness practices, such as gratitude and forgiveness. It also includes exploratory exercises for accessing the heart qualities of our deeper nature.

Practicing the Jhānas

Traditional Concentration

Meditation as Presented by the

Venerable Pa Auk Sayadaw

PAPERBACK • 978-1-59030-733-5 • $22.95

E-BOOK • 978-0-8348-2282-5 • $17.99

PUBLISHED DECEMBER 2009

COAUTHORED WITH TINA RASMUSSEN

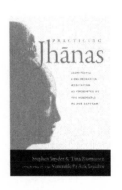

A clear and in-depth presentation of the traditional Theravada concentration meditation known as *jhāna* practice, developed from practicing *jhāna* meditation in retreat under the guidance of one of the great living meditation masters, the Venerable Pa Auk Sayadaw.

Made in the USA
Columbia, SC
24 September 2020